WHOM
I M

C000113633

WHOM SHALL
I MARRY?

Andrew Swanson

THE BANNER OF TRUTH TRUST

THE BANNER OF TRUTH TRUST
3 Murrayfield Road, Edinburgh EH12 6EL
P.O. Box 621, Carlisle, Pennsylvania 17013, USA

❋

© The Banner of Truth Trust 1995
First Published 1995
ISBN 0 85151 688 2

❋

Typeset in 10½/12pt Plantin Monotype
Printed in Great Britain by
BPC Paperbacks Ltd
A member of
The British Printing Company Ltd.

Contents

Whom Shall I Marry?

This is one of the most important questions you will ever think about. The fact that you have picked up this booklet and started to read it would suggest, at the very least, that it is a question which interests you. The first purpose of these pages is to draw attention to the scriptural teaching on this subject. Then I want to help Christians to see why it is very important that they use this teaching as their chief guide in choosing a marriage partner. At the present moment great damage is being done to the Christian church because there are many Christians who are either ignorant of this teaching or wilfully neglecting it. This ignorance or neglect is not confined to any particular nationality or culture. Sadly it is to be found in all nationalities and cultures. It is true to say, however, that some cultures have a greater tendency than others to increase the temptation to neglect this teaching. For example, in every culture where arranged marriages are the norm a powerful pressure will be exerted on Christians to ignore this teaching. This pressure is further increased when it is linked with the religious pressure of a non-Christian religion. Where, for instance, the national religion is mainly Muslim (even if there is a secular state) it will be very difficult for a convert from Islam to find a Christian partner from among his own people. Even should he find a suitable Christian partner there will usually be family pressure against the marriage.

The writer of this booklet is well aware of the peculiar difficulties and pressures that many young believers face when it comes to deciding whom they will marry. I have great sympathy with the dilemma that faces many converts from non-Christian religions when they try to find a suitable husband or wife. But the only satisfactory answer to this dilemma is one that is firmly based upon the teaching of Scripture. Every attempt to compromise the demands of Christian discipleship is bound to have unhappy consequences. On the other hand, no effort made to be faithful to Christ is too high a cost to pay for the blessing which is promised. I have no easy answer to the problems that confront many who will read these pages but I write under the conviction, 'them that honour me I will honour' (*1 Sam.* 2:30). Let us turn now and see what the Scriptures teach on this important subject.

The Starting Point
In 1 Corinthians chapters 6 and 7 the Apostle Paul twice reminds the Corinthians of a very basic Christian teaching. In chapter 6 verse 20 and chapter 7 verse 23 we are told, 'You were bought at a price'. This is something true, not just for the Corinthians of Paul's day but for every believer in every age. It is one of the most basic teachings of the Christian life. Every believer is the purchased possession of God. We have been redeemed, as Peter tells us, 'not with perishable things such as silver or gold ... but with the precious blood of Christ, a lamb without blemish or defect' (*1 Pet.* 1:18, 19). If you are a Christian you no longer have the undisputed right to do just as you choose. As Paul wrote to the Corinthians, 'you are not your own' (*1 Cor.* 6:19). Your body belongs to God: it is the temple of the Holy Spirit. This means you are not free to treat your body any way you choose to treat it. You are no longer to think of your body as your own to do with as you please. No! you

are to 'honour God with your body' (*1 Cor.* 6:20). In marriage you enter into the deepest possible union with another person. This means a Christian must always ask, 'Is this person I want to marry a person God permits me to marry?' Because you belong to God, you are simply not free to choose.

At the end of 1 Corinthians 7 Paul tells us the one primary qualification essential for a suitable marriage partner. Paul is talking about a widow who wishes to marry again but what he says equally applies to any Christian who wants to marry. This is what Paul says, 'If her husband dies, she is free to marry anyone she wishes, but *he must belong to the Lord.*' This is the most basic rule for Christian marriage. It is not the only thing that matters but it is the first thing. To put it as strongly and clearly as possible, the first question to be asked concerning a prospective marriage partner is, does he or she belong to Christ? If the answer to that question is 'Yes' then other questions can be considered. If the answer is 'No', then there is no need to ask any other questions. It is as if God speaks from heaven and tells you, 'This is not the person I want you to marry'.

Sad to say we are living in times when many people, Christians included, object to guidance that is as clear and straightforward as that. There are Christians today who are just like some of the leaders of Israel in Jeremiah's day. In a time of national calamity they came to Jeremiah and made this request: 'Pray that the Lord your God will tell us where we should go and what we should do.' This was a very good thing to do, and they went even further. They said to Jeremiah, 'May the Lord be a true and faithful witness against us if we do not act in accordance with everything the Lord your God sends you to tell us. Whether it is favourable or unfavourable, we will obey the Lord our God, to whom we are sending you, so that it will go well with us, for we will obey the Lord our God.' This is exactly the attitude Christians should have concerning the Word of God. Christians should be so committed to God's Word that they can honestly say, 'Whether it is favourable or unfavourable, we will obey the Lord our God.' The tragedy with the leaders of Jeremiah's day was their insincerity. When Jeremiah came with the Lord's Word they said, 'You are lying! the Lord our God has not sent you to say what you said' (*Jer.* 43:2).

Some Christians today act in almost exactly the same way. They say they want to do the Lord's will but when they are shown it and it is not what they want to do, they find a way of rejecting it. They will simply ignore God's Word. Some may try to argue that God's Word is not clear, or that, because some Christians give a different 'interpretation' we cannot be sure what God's will is. Yet others will agree that God's Word teaches they should not do what they are going to do; but, they say, God will understand their difficulties in keeping his Word. Even worse, there are some who will claim that they have prayed to God about the matter and he has given them an assurance that they are an exceptional case and it will be all right for them to do what other Christians should not do.

Now we all know there are some ethical problems about which it may be very difficult to be sure. We know that Christians may sincerely study God's Word and reach different conclusions on these matters. The issue we are considering does not belong to that category. This is a subject upon which God's Word speaks very clearly. There is one truly basic rule to guide every Christian in the choice of a marriage partner. It is a rule that gives most (but not all) Christians a great deal of discretion yet at the same time clearly forbids a certain class of people to be considered as suitable marriage partners. This is God's rule: any Christian is free to marry whom they wish, but the person must belong to the Lord. There is a remarkable similarity between this rule and the one and only commandment God gave to man before he sinned. God told Adam, 'You are free to eat from any tree in the garden: but you must not eat of the tree of the knowledge of good and evil' (*Gen.* 2:16, 17). This original command gives, on the one hand, plenty to choose from and, on the other hand, it singles out one tree, and only one forbidden tree whose fruit Adam must not eat. In the same way, God's rule for Christian marriage gives many believers a great choice of potential partner, while it unmistakably forbids a certain clearly defined class of people as suitable marriage partners for a Christian.

It could be argued that this rule will in effect leave some Christians with practically no choice of partner at all. For example, in lands where Islam or some other non-Christian religion holds sway, Christian converts are left with practically no choice. Their only choice would seem to be to marry an unbeliever or not to marry at all. While I have the deepest sympathy for a Christian convert facing the dilemma of wanting to marry yet having no suitable partner to marry, it is surely clear from Scripture that the rule still applies. It is God's rule and can only be broken with the most serious consequences. This rule is binding on the conscience of every Christian including those Christians who seem to be left with the choice of marrying a non-Christian or not marrying at all. Undoubtedly the temptation to bend the rule is great but it is in the best interests of the believer to resolve in his or her heart to resist this temptation.

Before you condemn the writer as heartless and insensitive let me remind you that I did not make the rule. It is God's rule we are thinking about, and, before we start arguing why God should make exceptions, there is an aspect of this rule that too many people never consider. It is assumed that in some situations the result will be that some believers will simply not be able to marry. The logic of this assumption is very simple:

The believer must not marry an unbeliever.

There are no believers to marry.

Therefore the believer cannot marry.

The logic may be sound and, in some cases, valid but it is a logic that ignores a very important point. It ignores the fact that God made this rule not to stop believers from being married but to prevent them marrying the wrong person.

When circumstances seem to suggest that some believers will not be able to marry because there are no suitable believers available there is no need for these believers to conclude their only hope for marriage is to disobey God and marry an unbeliever. Such a conclusion is simply the conclusion that comes when a believer listens to the 'father of lies'. It is to forget that the Christian has a heavenly Father who really does know what is best for his children. Every child of God needs to learn to bow in humble submission to the good and perfect will of their Father. We have a God who is concerned with much more than our material needs of 'clothing, food and drink' (see *Matthew* 6:32, 33). When Jesus assures us, 'your heavenly Father knows that ye need all these things', we can be assured he knows exactly what every single one of his children really needs.

Every child of God has a heavenly Father who delights, even more than any earthly father, to give good gifts to his children (see *Luke* 11:13). If our Father delights to give us his Holy Spirit why should we doubt his willingness and ability to give us other good gifts? Proverbs tells us, 'He who finds a wife finds a good thing, and obtains favour from the Lord.' Also, it tells us, 'Houses and riches are an inheritance from fathers, but a prudent wife is from the Lord' (*Prov.* 18:22; 19:14). The God who said, 'It is not good for man to be alone', was the God who provided Adam with 'a helper comparable [or suitable] to him' (*Gen.* 2:18). This God is the heavenly Father of every believer. And he can be trusted to provide everything that his wisdom sees will be good for his children. This is not to suggest the believer simply passively waits for God to bring a partner to him as he did with Adam. Proverbs implies activity on the part of the believer. It is the believer who *finds* but the Lord who *gives*. It is outside the scope of this booklet to make suggestions as to the believer's activity in finding a marriage partner, but I offer some guidelines later in this booklet. The only point that needs to be emphasised here is that the believer can trust God to provide and guide him to a suitable marriage partner if that is for the best.

This is a practical outworking of faith in a believer's life. God is concerned about every aspect of the life of his children and he wants his children to trust him. When a believer is in material need, would it cross his mind that maybe God would understand if he stole to meet his need? No! the believer would feel this was a call to more earnest waiting upon God to meet his need, or to learn contentment. The believer knows that God knows and cares about his material needs. The believer knows there is no way to justify stealing to provide for his need. Neither is there any way the believer can justify marrying an unbeliever. God expects us to trust his ability to provide a suitable marriage partner, or indeed to bless the believer who remains single. To encourage us in obedience God gives us a great variety of reasons why we should never fall to the temptation to marry an unbeliever or someone of another faith. Let's turn now and look at some of these reasons.

Why God Forbids Christians to Marry an Unbeliever

The most basic reason takes us back to the promise God made immediately after Adam and Eve fell into sin. Speaking to the serpent, God said, 'I will put enmity between you and the woman, and between your seed and her seed; he shall bruise your head, and you shall bruise his heel' (*Gen.* 3:15). When God says to the serpent that he will put enmity between his descendants and the descendants of the woman, he is saying that there will be continual conflict between Satan's children, as symbolised by the serpent's offspring or seed, and true believers, as symbolised by the woman's offspring. When Christ triumphed over Satan on Calvary, this conflict found its most dramatic fulfilment. For Jesus Christ is truly the offspring of the woman and the spiritual head of all believers.

As there is enmity between God's children and the children of the devil, there can be no real peace between these two 'seeds'. To marry an unbeliever is to marry a child of the devil. This may seem very strong language to describe an unbeliever but it is the language Jesus used to describe the unbelievers of his day. Why were the religious leaders of Jesus day wanting to kill Jesus? Because, as Jesus boldly told them, 'You are of your father the devil, and the desires of your father you want to do' (*John* 8:44). Later, in the same Gospel, Jesus went on to warn his disciples, 'If the world hates you, you know that it hated me before it hated you. If you were of the world, the world would love its own. Yet because you are not of the world, but I chose you out of the world, therefore the world hates you' (*John* 15:18, 19).

These words of Jesus need to be taken seriously. Jesus was not limiting these words to a certain class of unbeliever. He was not limiting it simply to the unbelievers who openly persecute his people. His words apply to every person in this world who is not a Christian. Their number includes some very nice, kindly, respectable, moral, church-going people. There are many non-Christian people who would hotly deny that they hate either Jesus or his people, but Jesus says they do. And he perfectly knows what is in their hearts. No professing Christian is free to hold a contrary opinion to their Lord and Saviour. So when Jesus tells us, 'the [unbelieving] world hates you', we had better believe it! More than that, we must think through the implications of this belief. Here are a few the reader will do well to ponder very carefully:

1. *Marriage to an unbeliever is marriage to a potential enemy for life.*

I have no wish to deny or even doubt that God in his mercy sometimes converts an unbelieving partner. I have witnessed this reality and am profoundly thankful to God that this occasionally takes place. But this does not alter the fact that, generally, unbelieving partners remain unconverted. As we will show shortly there is simply no certainty that an unbelieving partner will ever be converted. This means that whenever a believer marries an unbeliever there is the very real possibility of a life long partnership with a partner who will always be Christ's enemy. Sadly there are too many examples of disobedient believers who have found this out the hard way through bitter personal experience. They have gone into such a marriage in spite of the clear warnings of God's Word, perhaps hoping that their partner would be converted. Until they actually got married they had no idea of the trials that marriage to an unbeliever can bring. In many cases, they found out too late that the person they married was the enemy of their Lord and his people.

I am sure that many believers have been deceived into marriage by the false hope that their partner will get converted and so we want to make it quite clear this is a false hope. When the apostle Paul deals with the subject of marriage and divorce in 1 Corinthians 7, he envisages the possibility of an unbelieving partner, who, on the conversion of their spouse, wishes to separate (see verses 12–16). When this is the case Paul teaches, 'If the unbeliever leaves, let him do so. A believing man or woman is not bound in such circumstances' (v. 15). What does Paul mean by the expression, 'not bound in such circumstances'? He must mean that the believing partner is not obliged to try and stop the unbelieving partner leaving the marriage. The reason he gives in verse 15 is, 'God has called us to live in peace'. In other words, as Leon Morris helpfully explains, 'To cling to a marriage which the pagan is determined to end would inevitably lead to frustration and tension.'

Someone will argue that all the frustration and tension of trying to save the marriage would be worth it if the unbelieving partner were converted. Needless to say, this would be true, if such a result were sure. The apostle however makes it plain that such a result is by no means certain. This is what he goes on to write, 'How do you know, wife, whether you will save your husband? Or, how do you know, husband, whether you will save your wife?' To continue Morris's explanation, 'The certain strain is not justified by the uncertain result. Marriage should not be seen simply as an instrument of evangelism. The guiding principle must be "peace".'[1] If Paul pleads the uncertainty of conversion as a reason for a believer not clinging to a marriage his unbelieving partner is determined to end how much more

[1] L. Morris, *1 Corinthians, Tyndale New Testament Commentaries* (Leicester: IVP, 1985), p. 108. Other commentators, such as Charles Hodge, give a very different interpretation of 1 Corinthians 7:15, 16. While we believe that Morris' explanation is preferable, the fact remains that every interpretation of these verses must acknowledge the 'uncertainty of conversion'. On the one hand, Morris gives the more pessimistic interpretation of the 'uncertainty of conversion' whilst Hodge gives it an optimistic interpretation. The indisputable point, however, is the 'uncertainty of conversion'.

should 'the uncertainty of conversion' be a good reason for not entering into marriage with an unbeliever in the first place.

2. *Marriage with an unbeliever will constantly hinder your spiritual life.*

When God saw Adam's need for a partner in life the purpose of such a partner was summed up in the expression a 'suitable helper' (*Gen.* 2:20 NIV). This expression aptly describes a major purpose for both partners in a marriage. The Husband should be a 'suitable helper' for his wife and the wife should be a 'suitable helper' for her husband. The husband needs a partner who will provide help that is suitable to his particular needs. He needs a companion with whom he can share his life, someone he can love, confide in and trust, someone he can discuss things with, someone he enjoys being with. He needs a homemaker who will superintend the smooth running of the home, and a mother who will provide the maternal care the children need. But especially he needs someone who will be a real help to him in his spiritual life; someone who is concerned for his spiritual well-being and who will pray for him and discuss spiritual matters with him and offer spiritual counsel.

Similarly, the wife needs a partner who will provide help suitable to her particular needs. She needs a husband who will help her to be a good wife and who will help her to be a good housekeeper and mother; but more especially she needs a husband who can help in these ways because he is a spiritual man, sharing with his wife a faith in Jesus Christ. Only a Christian man can give the kind of help a Christian woman needs. Only a Christian woman can give the kind of help a Christian man needs. This is the basic requirement for a suitable marriage partner. There may be many other things that a man or woman looks for in a prospective marriage partner. It is not wrong to wish for someone you find attractive, who shares similar interests or a similar background. These and many other qualifications have some importance in guiding your choice of a marriage partner. The one qualification, however, that is a must as opposed to an optional extra is that the prospective partner really shares your Christian faith.

If your prospective partner is good looking, has a secure occupation, shares many of your interests and whatever else you value – that is a bonus not to be despised. But these matters are not of first importance. They must never replace the one thing that really matters. If a prospective partner has everything you ever wished for and is not a believer, forget it! Be assured, nothing good can come from marrying such a person. That person is not God's choice for you. This temptation must be resisted.

Do not mistake what I am saying! I am not saying that a common faith is *all* that really matters. I am not saying find a believer and you have found God's choice of partner for you. All I am saying is that a prospective partner *must* really share your Christian faith. Whatever else they have or have not, the one essential qualification is a common faith. The reason for this is simply that *only* those who have this qualification can have any hope of being a help suitable to you.

This point is so vital it deserves further practical consideration. Try to imagine the difficulties of taking your faith seriously with a partner who does not share your spiritual convictions. Consider a few examples. If you are a Christian you will want to be closely involved in the life and witness of a local church. You will obviously want to attend the Sunday and midweek services. It is right that you should but think how unpleasant life will be if your partner does not share your sense of commitment to these things. Either you will go alone to some or all of these meetings or you will be aware that your partner resents your involvement in something he (or she) cannot enjoy. Do you really want to spend a lifetime in partnership with someone who cannot share the most important thing in your life?

If you are a Christian you will rightly want to bring your children up in the Christian faith. Even with the most understanding of unbelieving partners this will prove immensely difficult. Whether you like it or not, your children will have conflicting examples to follow. However closely you seek to follow the Lord, and however faithful you are in seeking to instruct your children in the ways of God, there will always be the neutralising influence of the unbelieving partner. Whenever your children need discipline this will be difficult to enforce consistently if your partner does not share your convictions about the need for biblical standards of discipline. It will be confusing for your children when they recognise the different standards of each of their parents. You will have constant conflicts with your partner because you are seeking to please the Lord, and your partner has no higher principle than to please you.

We could easily multiply examples of ways in which an unbelieving partner (even a kind caring co-operative one) hinders the spiritual life of the believing partner; but turning from more negative aspects of this subject let us now look at it more positively.

Why the Believer Should Only Marry in the Lord.

1. *Only the union of two believers can achieve the aims of Christian marriage.*
Christian marriage is intended to show marriage as God meant it to be. It is intended to be something that displays what real love can achieve. It is a relationship that is intended to grow and develop over the years. Supremely it is a life-long commitment of two people to love each other

and to help each other live to the glory of God. Together they achieve that pattern of marital love and fulfilment which Paul describes as 'a great mystery' (*Eph.* 5:32). The marriage relationship is intended to be a visual aid to the world of the wonderful relationship that exists between Christ and his Church. The Apostle Paul works out the details of this so clearly in Ephesians 5:22–33. As you study this passage carefully, you will see the impossibility of achieving this goal when only one partner is a believer. When both partners are believers seeking to live up to their marriage responsibilities, they help each other. There is simply no way that such a commitment can be kept by a couple that are not united in the Lord.

Notice that after Paul has written about marriage, he goes on to write about parent-child and employer-employee relationships. Immediately after this, in Ephesians 6:10-20 he deals with the spiritual warfare. Why is this? He wants us to see that these areas of our lives are under attack from the powers of darkness. Satan and his evil hosts hate human relations to work out as God intends. They hate God's order and they seek to do all they can to destroy it. If you have two believers striving to order their marriage according to God's intention, they are united in resisting Satan's endeavours to ruin God's order. If one of the partners is already on Satan's side, God's order has been broken and there is no way the marriage can fulfil the full purpose of Christian marriage.

I have already pointed out how much more difficult it is to bring up children as God intends when the parents are pulling in different directions. There is no doubt that God can raise up Christian children out of non-Christian homes. He can also raise them out of homes where only one parent is a Christian. We thank God that he is able to do this and that he does! However, God generally chooses to raise Christian children through the means of their being brought up under the influence of Christian parents. Christians who wish to get married should be thinking seriously about the possibility of parenthood. It is most likely that children will grow up to be like their parents. Subconsciously they will model themselves on the example set by their mother or father. Christians thinking of marriage should look for someone who will be a good example for their children to follow. Any Christian who seriously thinks like this could never consider a non-Christian suitable as a marriage partner. There are non-Christians who live good lives but their example would not (and could not) teach your children to love God and put Him first.

Another major aim of Christian marriage is the witness of a Christian home to the world. Few Christians fully realise the potential for good to the world through the example and witness of a truly Christian home: a home where the husband and wife seek to live as God intends, with both partners committed to honouring God in all their relationships. Many previously unchurched people have been brought into contact with evangelical churches in the first instance through the warm witness of a Christian home. It takes little imagination to see the problems and difficulties of trying to use the home in this way when only one partner is a Christian. If you want your marriage to be the blessing to others that God means it to be, be sure you marry someone who shares this concern. You have no right to expect God to bless your marriage to others if you have married in disobedience to God's express command that you marry 'only in the Lord'.

2. *Marriage to a believer is one of the ways you can glorify the Lord.* The great question for every believer is, how can I best live to please God? The Apostle Paul teaches us that our whole life should be governed by the principle, 'whatever you do,

do it all for the glory of God' (*1 Cor.* 10:31). In the context in which Paul writes these words, he is emphasising the fact that even our eating and drinking should be controlled by this principle. He is clearly teaching that we can and ought to seek to glorify God in the things we allow ourselves to eat and drink. But that is only one example of the principle. It is not just that God expects us to glorify him in what we eat or drink but also, 'whatever you do, do it all for the glory of God'. This means that every believer who contemplates marriage ought to ask, 'Can I be married to the glory of God?'

Believers should never simply get married because they want to be married or because they feel pressurised into being married. No! believers should only marry if they can marry to the glory of God. Believers should be thinking of the purpose that God intends marriage to fulfil. Unless the believer is willing to make God's purpose for marriage his or her own, he or she will not be able to glorify God in marriage. For example if a man is not prepared to enter marriage with the intention of loving his wife 'as Christ loves the Church' (*Eph.* 5:25) he will not be able to marry to the glory of God.

Christian marriage is marriage for life (*Matt.* 19:6) and no Christian can please God in his marriage unless there is a sincere commitment to a life-long relationship of faithful marriage. Christians cannot marry to the glory of God if they have any mental reservations about this life-long commitment. They cannot marry to the glory of God if they have any thoughts of the possibility of their marriage being dissolved if things do not work out.

3. *Marriage to a believer is an outward evidence of your love to the Lord.*
Jesus told his disciples, 'If you love me you will obey what I command'. 'Whoever has my commands and obeys them,

he is the one who loves me'. 'If anyone loves me, he will obey my teaching'. 'He who does not love me will not obey my teaching' (*John* 14:15, 21, 23–24). Jesus is clearly teaching that the real evidence of a believer's love for him is their obedience to his teaching. Jesus commanded his disciples to 'go and make disciples of all nations, baptising them in the name of the Father and of the Son and of the Holy Spirit, and teaching them to obey everything I have commanded you' (*Matt.* 28:19, 20). Jesus does not limit his commands to those he spoke with his own mouth; he includes the commands spoken in his name by his chosen apostles. When Paul wrote, 'she is free to marry anyone she wishes, but he must belong to the Lord', he was giving a command from the Lord. Paul was not expressing his own opinion on the subject or merely giving advice. He was giving us the mind of the Lord on this subject.

The great longing of every true believer is to please his Lord and Saviour Jesus Christ. For the believer the Lord's commands are not burdensome (*1 John* 5:3). They are not just an expression of his sovereign right to direct our lives. They are much more than that. They are an expression of his loving wisdom. He forbids us nothing that is really good for us and when he forbids us anything we may be sure he does it in our best interests. He knows the fearful trials and dangers to the soul that marriage to an unbeliever will bring and for our good he forbids such folly. In doing so he gives every believer an opportunity of responding to his love by keeping his commandment. For some believers this will mean waiting a long time for the right partner. For others it may even mean remaining single for life. But for every true believer their willingness to marry only in the Lord, or not to marry at all, are Saviour-given opportunities to show the reality of their love for him. Remember whatever sacrifice you may make, it pales into insignificance when we consider, 'that though he was rich, yet for your sakes he became poor, so that you through his poverty might become rich' (*2 Cor.* 8:9).

Some True Testimonies

Marriage to an unbeliever is marriage to a potential enemy for life (page 15)

1. Ali is a young man from a Middle Eastern Village. His father is a very devout Muslim, so when Ali became a believer in Jesus, he told the rest of his family but not his father. When it was time for him to marry, he could not tell his father that he did not want a Muslim wife. He said he must have a girl who did not cover her head. The engagement went ahead, and when Ali's believing friends warned him he assured them that the girl was not a strong Muslim. After they were married, he was sure, if he were a good loving husband she would see this came from his faith and she would believe too.

Ali was married nearly two years ago and they have been very hard years. He has to work long hours to provide for his wife and now his son and, in the little free time that he has, his wife rightly wants his attention. He is never able to meet with his believing friends to worship. His wife has never shown any interest in his faith and he is a very sad man.

2. Mark was popular. He was a shining example of the Christian student, always keen to discuss his faith and what God meant to him. His flat was used for Bible study groups and many Christians were helped by his wise advice. Kate was much younger than the others and she often wept on his shoulder, 'wishing' that she was converted. He tried to help her, spending more and more time alone with her. Eventually they were married and Kate's interest in

salvation evaporated. Mark's spiritual growth was stunted. His home was now closed to his Christian friends. He carried on attending the same church, but suffered from a lack of wider spiritual fellowship. When their family became rebellious teenagers, Kate mellowed a little and returned to church with him. Her earlier interest in salvation has re-kindled, and she is more welcoming to Mark's friends.

Marriage to a believer is one of the ways you can glorify the Lord (page 21)

1. Gülsen is a young Muslim who has become a Christian. She is shortly to marry a Christian from a Middle Eastern country and this will mean her leaving her family and country, but it is very important for her to be sharing her life with another Christian. She and her friends were talking recently about some believers who have married unbelievers and she was amazed. She said, 'Since I have become a Christian, I want to be with other Christians. Even though I love my mother, I find it hard to share the home with her and to see the books she reads, for example. How can a believer choose to spend the rest of his life in a home with an unbeliever? It is unthinkable.' She is right.

2. Tony and Jane decided very quickly that they wanted to marry and start a family. They were young, cheerful and well matched in many ways, encouraging each other in their faith. Two to three years after their marriage they were still childless. Following various tests it was confirmed that, as a couple, they were sterile. They felt devastated. After the initial shock they began to look again at their life plans and sought God's direction for them as a couple. Their marriage has been strengthened and their faith enormously increased as a result. Their welcoming home reflects the peace, harmony and fulfilment of a true Christian marriage.

Only the union of two believers can achieve the aims of Christian marriage (page 19)

Moira and James were an ill-matched pair. During one long vacation she worked as a waitress in a city centre hotel. James was twenty years older, bitter and lonely. She was a back-slidden Christian that summer, but her naturally caring and friendly personality reached out to the lonely middle-aged man. Soon she was involved with him, going for outings together on her days off. She assured her friends and concerned parents (and probably herself too) that there was nothing in it – she was just being friendly. James did not see it that way. Within two years, against (maybe in spite of) clear Christian teaching not to marry an un-believer, Moira married James. She has lived to regret it. There is a major conflict in disciplining the children. She sees Christian friends whose marriages reflect the union of Christ and the church, but in her own marriage there are tensions. She is alone, unable to share her deepest feelings of faith with her partner. She prays faithfully for him to come to salvation, but she strongly cautions every Christian against binding themselves in an ungodly marriage.

Marriage to a believer is an outward evidence of your love to the Lord (page 22)

When Fatma was about seventeen years old, she was so miserable she planned to commit suicide while her family were away from the house. Just at that time, Kaan, a family friend, arrived and saved her from her intention. After that there was an understanding between Kaan and Fatma that they would marry some time in the future.

However, Fatma became a believer in the Lord Jesus. For a long time she still loved Kaan in her heart and argued that it would be a bad witness to break her word to him. Later she realised that marriage to an unbeliever would not be right but she still loved Kaan and so prayed for him to believe too. Eventually, she began to change her prayer and ask the Lord to take away her love for Kaan, something which she thought was impossible. Now she is praying that, in God's time, He will provide her with a strong, believing husband so that they can share their lives together according to God's Word and be witnesses to the world around.

Did You Err?

This booklet may well be read by some who know from bitter experience the mistake which it is aimed at helping Christians to avoid. Some may have simply entered marriage with little or no understanding of the biblical teaching on this subject. Others, perhaps, knew the teaching but were deceived into thinking that they were an exception and went into marriage hoping that their partner would eventually become a Christian. Yet others may have married thinking that their partner was a believer and discovered that this was not the case. Finally, there may be those who have become Christian since their marriage. We have the deepest sympathy for those who belong to any one of these categories and we wish to close this booklet with a few words of counsel and encouragement.

First of all, whatever category you fall into, the great truth to hold on to is that your situation is not out of God's control. Whether your situation is very much of your own making or whether little or no blame attaches to you, never forget that your situation is known perfectly to God. If you are a believer you must take comfort from the knowledge that your situation (with all its sorrows and pain) is one of the 'all things' that 'work together for good to those who love God' (*Rom.* 8:28). Do not give in to despair or self-pity. Do not resign yourself to a hopeless future.

Secondly, always remember that 'there is forgiveness with God, that he may be feared' (*Psa.* 130:4). If your conscience tells you that you have only yourself to blame for your present situation, take heed and confess this to the Lord. Be honest with God. Do not waste your time trying to excuse your sin. Tell him that you are sorry, and seek his forgiveness.

Thirdly, never forget that God can completely change your situation. When you pray for this, begin by asking that God will change your attitude to your situation. Pray that God will use your difficult situation to change you yourself. Pray that in spite of everything you will become a better husband or wife, father or mother. Pray that God will give you the patience, wisdom, love and every grace you need to fulfil your God-given responsibilities to your partner. In this way you will commend the gospel of God's grace to your partner in the best way possible. Finally, never stop praying for your partner's conversion and never give up hope that God is able to answer this prayer.

If Christians disobey the revealed will of God, either through ignorance or wilfully, they can expect to experience the chastening hand of God. However, the same love that chastens not only forgives the repentant believer's folly but sometimes even gives them the desire of their heart and converts their partner. The writer knows of a couple who were refused marriage in a church because one of them, a believer, was marrying an unbeliever. The couple found someone else to marry them and for some years there was a marriage that was less than the Christian ideal. During these years God dealt with both partners and the unbeliever was converted. Thank God he graciously does such things but never forget that there may be years of painful chastening before he does.

The Believer's Role in Finding a Marriage Partner

As already stated, the scope of this book forbids any detailed treatment of this important subject. However, the publishers felt that these additional pages listing a few broad biblical guidelines might prove helpful.

1. In seeking a marriage partner, the first rule to observe is: 'seek first the kingdom of God and his righteousness' (*Matt.* 6:33). In other words, never allow yourself to become preoccupied with the importance of finding a marriage partner. Do not allow this matter, however important, to become the priority of your life. This is the great mistake that so many make. Avoid it by making God's priority yours. Trust God to look after your material needs and all these other things (marriage, if it is good for you) 'shall be added unto you.'

2. With God's help prepare yourself to be the best possible marriage partner. Remember that you are a son or daughter of the King. When the King chooses to give you another of his sons or daughters as a marriage partner, see that you have all the attractions that ought to be seen in those of royal descent. This thought could be illustrated in so many ways but let two examples suffice.

(a) Let the whole of your life be seen to be controlled by your concern for the glory of God. The kind of partner that will be suitable for you will be the kind of partner that recognises and appreciates someone who is seeking first the Kingdom of God and his righteousness. Aim to be a man or woman of prayer, one who delights to walk closely with God, one who delights to walk in the ways of God. Let your whole life reflect the reality that you are a son or daughter of the King.

(b) Study God's Word to see the kind of character God wants you to be. See what God thinks is important. If you are a woman, ask God to clothe you with the beauty of a 'meek and quiet spirit.' If you are a man, ask God to give you the ability to understand and readiness to meet all the spiritual, intellectual, emotional and material needs of a person whom God's Word describes as 'the weaker vessel' (see *1 Peter* 3:1-7). Ask God to show you those things that ought to please a suitable marriage partner and ask God to help you cultivate these qualities.

3. Make sure you know how to recognise a true believer. Do not be taken in by appearances. Ask God to give you spiritual discernment. Ask him to show you what to look for. Ask questions. Does this person love God's Word, his day, his people? Can you see the fruit of the Spirit in this life? (see *Galatians* 5:22–23). Does this person pray, talk of spiritual things, live a life of faith?

4. As you have opportunity, go to the places where you would expect to meet a Christian partner. Seek to be open and friendly but avoid any appearance of hunting for a partner.

5. Finally, make this whole matter a continual dialogue with God. 'Trust in the Lord with all your heart and lean not to your own understanding; in all your ways acknowledge him and he shall direct your paths' (*Prov.* 3:5, 6).